The Greatest of All Time: Leonardo Da Vinci

Preface

If I was talking about a man called Da Vinci. Would you recognize him?

"Yes, the one who painted Mona Lisa."

But Da Vinci means 'from Vinci!'

So, who's Da Vinci?

Leonardo di ser Piero da Vinci (5 April 1452 – 2 May 1519) was an Italian polymath* of 14th century belonging to the Italian Renaissance period. He was brilliant in Inventing, drawing, painting, sculpting, architecture, science, music, mathematic, engineering, literature, anatomy, geology, astronomy, botany, zoology, writing, history, physiology, histology, embryology and cartography. He has been called the father of palaeontology, ichnology, architecture and painting. He is considered as the best painter of all time. He is the one who created the concept of parachute, helicopter and tank. He epitomised the **Renaissance humanist** ideal. Many scholars regard Leonardo as the "Universal Genius" and "feverishly inventive imagination". He is considered as the most talented individual ever lived. the scope and depth of his interests were without precedent in recorded history. "his mind and personality seem to us superhuman, while the man himself mysterious and remote" told an art historian Helen Gardener. Marco Rosci notes that, while there is much speculation regarding his life and personality, his view of the world was logical rather than mysterious, although the empirical methods he employed were unconventional for his time.

> * is a person whose expertise spans a significant number of subject areas, known to draw on complex bodies of knowledge to solve specific problems.

Childhood

Leonardo was born on 15th of April 1452 at the third hour of the night in Tuscan hill town of Vinci, in the lower valley of the Arno river in Republic of Florence. He was out of a wedlock named caterina and son of the wealthy Messer Piero Fruosino di Antonio da Vinci, a Florentine legal notary. Leonardo had no surname in modern sense. His full name was Leonardo di ser Piero da Vinci which means Leonardo, (son) of (ser)Piero from Vinci. "ser" indicated shows that his father was a gentleman. More about his early life is unknown. He spend his 5 years in Hamlet of Anchiano (village near Vinci) in home of his mother, and from 1457 lived with his father, grandparents, and Uncle in a small house in Vinci. Later his father married a 16year old girl named Albiera Amadori, who loved Leonardo but died Young, In 1465 without children. When Leonardo was 16 years his father married again 25-year-old Francesca Lanfredini, who also died without kids. Piero's Legitimate heir was born from his 3rd Margherita di Guglielmo (who gave birth to 6 children) and his 4th and final wife Lucrezia Cortigiani (who also gave birth to 6 children).

In all Leonardo had total of 12 half-siblings, who were so younger then him (in fact Leonardo's last sibling was born when Leonardo was 40 years old). Leonardo had very few contacts with his Half-siblings and Step-Mothers because they cause him difficulties after his father's death in dispute of inheritance.

Leonardo received an informal Education in Latin, geometry and mathematics.

Vasari, a 16th century biographer tells a story of Leonardo as a young man A local peasant made himself a round shield and requested that Ser Piero have it painted for him. Leonardo responded with a **painting of a monster** spitting fire that was so terrifying that Ser Piero sold it to a Florentine art dealer, who sold it to the **Duke of Milan**. Meanwhile, having made a profit, Ser Piero bought a shield decorated with a heart pierced by an arrow, which he gave to the peasant.

Physical Characteristics

Descriptions and portraits of Leonardo create an image of a man who was tall for his time & place. He was extremely handsome. He was at least 5'8" according his length of skeleton. His portrait indicates that as an old man, he had long hair, at the time most men wore cropped short. His hair reached his Shoulders. When most men prefer Clean-shave or short beard, Leonardo's beard flow till his chest.

His clothing was described being unusual in his choice of bright colors. At his time when most mature men wear long garments, Leonardo's preferred outfit was short Tunic and hose generally worn by younger men.

Vasari's description

As said by Vasari "In the normal course of events many men and women are both with various remarkable qualities & talents; but occasionally, in a way that transcends nature, a single person is marvelously endowed by heaven with beauty, grace and talent in such abundance that he leaves other men far behind… Everyone admitted that this was true of Leonardo da Vinci, an artist of outstanding physical beauty who displayed infinite grace in everything he did and who cultivated his genius so brilliantly that all problems he studied were solved with ease. He possessed great strength and dexterity; he was a man of regal spirit and tremendous breadth of mind..."

Left-Handed

It has been written that Leonardo "may be the most universally recognized left-handed artist of all-time", a fact documented by various Renaissance authors and manifested conspiracy in his drawing and handwriting. In his notebook he wrote in mirror image because it was easier for him, he was falsely accused for trying to protect his work.

Portraits

Leonardo's face is best known from a drawing in red chalk that appears to be self-portrait. However, they were some controversy over the identity of the subject, because the man represented appeared to be greater than 67 in age.

Character

Leonardo da Vinci was described by his early biographers as a man with great personal appeal, kindness, and generosity. He was generally loved by his fellow.

According to Vasari "Leonardo's disposition was so lovable that he commanded everyone's affection". He was a "sparkling conversationalist" Who charmed Ludovico il Moro with his intelligence. Vasari sums him up by saying: "In appearance he was striking and handsome, and his magnificent presence brought comfort to the most troubled soul; he was so persuasive that he could bend other people to his will. He was physically so strong that he could withstand violence and with his right hand he could bend the ring of an iron door knocker or a horseshoe as if they were led. He was so generous that he fed all his friends, rich or poor.... Through his birth Florence received a very great gift, and through his death it sustained an incalculable loss."

Some of Leonardo's Philosophies can be found in a series of fable that he wrote.

Little is known about Leonardo's intimate relationships from his own writing. Some evidence of Leonardo's personal relationships emerges both from historic records and his writings of his many biographers.

Verrocchio's workshop

In 1466, at the age of 14, Leonardo was apprenticed to the artist Andreas di Cione, known as Verrocchio, whose workshop was finest in Florence. HE appeals as a studio boy to Andreas di

Verrocchio, the leading Florentine Painter and sculpture of the day (and would do so for 7 years). other painters would associate with Domenico, Perugino, Botticelli and Lorenzo di Credi. Leonardo was exposed to both theoretical learning and vast range of technical skills. Including drafting, chemistry, metal working, plaster casting, leather working, painting, sculpting and modeling. Much of Verrocchio's production was done by his employees. According to Vasari, Leonardo collaborated with Verrocchio on his The Baptism of Christ, painting young angel holding Jesus' robe in a manner that was so far supercilious to his master's that Verrocchio put down his brush and never painted again. Leonardo may have been model for 2 works by Verrocchio: The brown statue of David and the Archangel Raphael in Tobias and the Angel.

Florence at the time of Leonardo's youth was the heart of Christian humanist thought and culture. Leonardo commenced his apprenticeship with Verrocchio in 1466, the year that Verrocchio's master, the great sculpture Donatello, died. The painter Uccello, whose early experiments with perspective were to influence the development of the landscape painting, was a very old man. The painter Piero Della Francesca & Filippo Lippi, sculptor Luca Della Robia, and architect and writer Leon Battista Alberti were in their sixties. The successful artists of the next generation were Leonardo's teachers Verrocchio, Antonio del Pullaiuolo, and the portrait sculptor Mino da Fiesole. The latter's life like busts give the most reliable likenesses of Lorenzo Medici's father Piero and uncle Giovanni.

By 1472 at the age of 20, Leonardo was qualified as a master in the Guild of the Saint Luke, the guild of artist and Doctor of Medicine. Later Leonardo's father set him up a workshop, still his attachment with Verrocchio continued to collaborate with him. Leonardo's earliest known dated is work in a pen and ink of the Arno valley, drawn on 5th August 1473.

Personal Relationship

Pupil

Leonardo maintained enduring relationship with 2 pupils who were apprenticed to him as children. These were Gian Giacomo Capprotti da Oreno, who entered his household in 1490 at the age of 10, and count Francesco Melzi, the son of a Milan aristocrat who was apprenticed to his father in 1506, at the age of 14, remaining with his until his death.

Gian Giacomo was nicknamed Salai or il Salaino sense "the little Devil". Vasari defines him as "a graceful and beautiful youth with fine curly hair". The "little devil" lived up to his nickname: a year after his entering the household Leonardo made a list of the boy's crimes, calling him a 'thief, a lair, stubborn and a greedy gut". But despite Salai's thievery and general delinquency – he made off with money and valuables on at least 5 occasions, spent a fortune on apparel, including 24 pairs of shoes, and eventually died in duel – he remained Leonardo's servant, and assistant for 30 years. At Leonardo's death he bequeathed the Mona Lisa, a valuable price even then, valued in Salai's own will at equivalent of £200,000.

Melzi escorted Leonardo in his final days in France. On Leonardo's death he wrote a letter to inform Leonardo's brothers, describing him as "like an excellent father to me" and goes on to say: "Everyone is grieved at the loss of such man that Nature no longer has it in her power to produce. Melzi played an important role as a guardian of Leonardo's notebook, preparing them for publication in the form directed by the master, but was not to see project realized.

Little is revealed about Leonardo's sexuality, as, although he left 100s' of pages of writing, very little of it is personal in nature. He left no letters, poetry or diary that indicate romantic interest. He never married but it is said that he had secret affair with La Gioconda or popularly known as Mona Lisa.

The only historical document concerning Leonardo's sexual life is accusation of sodomy made in 1476, while he was still in Verrocchio's workshop.

Michael White points out that willingness to discuss aspects of Leonardo's sexual identity has varied according to contemporary attitudes. His near-contemporary biographer Vasari makes no reference to Leonardo's sexuality whatsoever. In the 20th century biographers made explicit reference to a probability that Leonardo.

Patrons, Friends & Colleague

Leonardo da Vinci had several powerful patrons, including the King of France. He had, over the years, a large number of followers and pupils.

- His patrons included the Medici, Ludovico Sforza and Cesare Borgia, in whose service he spent the years 1502 & 1503 And King Francis I of France.

- He had working relation with two other notable scientists, Luca Pacioli & Marcantonio Della Torre and was a close friend of Niccolò Machiavelli.

- He had a close, long-lasting friendship with Isabella d'Este, a renowned patroness of the arts, whose portrait he drew while on a Journey that took him through Mantua.

- The de Predis brothers & collaboration on Virgin of the Rocks.

- His relationships with Michelangelo was always tense and ambivalent, as the two had such contrasting characters.

Fame & Reputation

Leonardo's fame within his own lifetime was such that king of France carried him like a Trophy and claimed to support him in his old age and held him in his arms as Leonardo died. Everyone continued to admire his paintings & sculptor. He inspired many individuals to write books.

By 19th century the scope of Leonardo's notebook was known as well as his paintings. Hippolyte Taine wrote in 1866: "There may not be in the world an example of another genius so universal, so incapable of fulfilment, so full of yearning for the infinite, so naturally refined so far ahead of his own century and the following centuries." Art historian Bernard Berenson wrote in 1896: "Leonardo is the one artist of whom it may be said with perfect literalness: Nothing that he touched but turned into a thing of eternal beauty. Whether it be the cross section of a skull, the structure of a weed, or a study of muscles, he, with his feeling for line and for light and shade, forever transmuted it into life-communicating values."

Interest

Vasari says of the child Leonardo "He would have been very proficient in his early lessons, if he had not been so volatile and flexible; for he was always setting himself to learn a multitude of things, most of which were shortly abandoned. When he began the study of arithmetic, he made, within a few months, such remarkable progress that he could baffle his master with the questions and problems that he raised... All the time, through all his other enterprises, Leonardo never ceased drawing..."

Music Ability

It appears from Vasari's description that Leonardo first learned to play the lye as a child and that he was very talented at improvisation. In about 1479 he created a lyre in the shape of a horse's head, which was made "mostly of silver", and of "sonorous and resonant" tone. Lorenzo de' Medici saw this lyre and wishing to better his relationship with Ludovico Sforza, the usurping Duke of Milan, he sent Leonardo to present this lyre to the Duke as a gift. Leonardo's musical performances so far surpassed those of Ludovico's court musicians that the Duke was delighted.

Love of Nature

Leonardo always loved nature. One of the reasons was because of his childhood environment. Near his childhood house were mountains, trees, and rivers. There were also many animals. This environment gave him the perfect chance to study the surrounding area; it also may have encouraged him to have interest in painting. Later in life he recalls his exploration of an ominous cavern in the mountains as formative.

Science Inventions of Leonardo Da Vinci

Leonardo renowned In fields of civil engineering, chemistry, geometry, hydrodynamics, geology, mathematics, aerodynamics, physics, mechanical engineer, optic, pyrotechnics & zoology.

His scientific studies & theories are only capable of understanding in last 150 years. As an engineer, Leonardo convinced ideas vastly ahead of his time. He gave the concept of parachute improved version of helicopter, armored fighting vehicle, solar power, calculator and theory of double hull. He advanced great knowledge in anatomy, astronomy, physics, optics, aerodynamics & hydrodynamics.

Approach of Scientific Investigation

During the Renaissance study of Science was not perceived as mutually exclusive; on the contrary, the one was informing upon the other. Although Leonardo's training was primarily as an artist, it was largely through his scientific approach to the art of painting, and his development of a style that coupled his scientific knowledge with his unique ability to render what he saw that created the outstanding masterpieces of art for which he is famous.

As a scientist Leonardo received no formal education in Latin and Mathematic and did not attend university. Because of these reasons his studies were largely overlooked by scholars. Leonardo's approach to science was intense level of observation and recording, his tools of investigations was entirely his Eyes.

Leonardo's notes & Journals

Leonardo kept a series of Journals in which he wrote almost daily, as well as separate notes and sheets of observation, comments and plans. He wrote and drew with his left hand and most of his scripts is in mirror scripts which makes it difficult to read. Much has survived to illustrate Leonardo's studies, discoveries and inventions.

On his death he left his notes to his pupil Melzi with apparent intention that his scientific work should be published. This did not happen in Melzi's lifetime, and the writings were eventually bound in difference forms and dispersed. Some of his works were published as a treatise on painting after 165 years after his death.

Publication

Leonardo illustrated a book on mathematical proportion in art written by his friend Luca Pacioli and called da divina proportione, published in 1509. He was also preparing a major treatise on his scientific observations and mechanical invention. It was to be divided into several sections or "Books", Leonardo leaving some instructions as to how they were to be ordered. Many sections of it appeared in his notebook.

These pages deal with scientific subjects like specifically as they touch upon his creation of artworks. In relating to art, this is not science that dependent upon experimenting of theories.

Natural Science

Light

Leonardo wrote:

The light which may illuminate opaque bodies of 4 kinds. These are; diffused light as that of the atmosphere; And Direct, as that of the sun; The third is Reflected Light; and there is 4th Which can pass through bodies (translucent) bodies, as the paper or linen etc.

For an artist working in 15th century, some study of light was important. It was by the effective painting of light falling on that modelling, or a 3-dimentional appearance was to be achieved in a 2-dimension medium. It was also understood by artist like Leonardo's teacher, Verrocchio, that an appearance of space and distance could be achieved in a background landscape of by painting in tones that were less in contrast and colors that were less bright than in foreground of the painting. The effect of light on solids were achieved by trial and error, since few artists except Piero Della Francesca had accurate knowledge of the subject.

At the time Leonardo commenced painting, it was unusual for figures to be painted with extreme contrast of light and shade. Faces were shadowed in a manner that was bland and maintained all the features and contours clearly visible. Leonardo broke with this. In the painting generally titled "The lady with Ermine" (1483) he sets figure diagonally to the picture space and turns her head so that her face is almost parallel to the to her nearer shoulder. The back of her head and the further shoulder are deeply shadowed. Around the ovoid solid of her head and across her breast and hand the light is diffused in such a way that the distance and position of light in relation to the figure can be calculated.

Leonardo's treatment of light in painting such as "The Virgin of the Rocks" and "Mona Lisa" was to change forever the way in which the artist perceives light and used it in their painting. Of all Leonardo's scientific legacies, this is probably the one that had the most immediate and noticeable effect.

Human Anatomy

Leonardo wrote:

...to obtain a true and perfect knowledge ... I have dissected more than ten human bodies, destroying all the other members, and removing the very minutest particles of the flesh by which these veins are surrounded, ... and as one single body would not last so long, since it was necessary to proceed with several bodies by degrees, until I came to an end and had a complete knowledge; this I repeated twice, to learn the differences...

Topography Anatomy

Leonardo commenced the formal study of anatomy of the Human Body when apprenticed to Verrocchio. As a student he would have been taught to draw human body from life, to memorize the muscles, tendons and visible subcutaneous structure and to familiarize himself with the mechanics of various parts of the skeleton and muscular structure. It was common workshop practice to have plasters casts of parts of human available for students to study and draw.

Leonardo is the one who painted arms and Torso Christ in "The Baptism of Christ" on which he famously collaborated with his master Verrocchio, then his understanding of topographical anatomy had surpassed that of his master at an early age as can be seem by comparison of the arms of Christ with those of "John the Baptist" in the same painting.

In 1490s he wrote about demonstrating muscle and sinews to students:

> Remember that to be certain of the point on origin of any muscle, you must pull the sinew from which the muscle springs in such a way as to see that muscle move, and where it is attached to the ligaments of the bones.

He continued his investigation in this field occupied many pages of notes, each dealing systematically with an aspect of anatomy. It appears that the notes were intended for publication, a task entrusted on his death his Melzi.

In conjunction with studies of aspects of body are drawings of faces displaying different emotions and many drawings of people suffering facial deformity, either congenital or though illness. Some of these drawings, generally referred to as "caricatures", on analysis of skeleton proportions, appear to be based on anatomical studies.

Dissection

As Leonardo became successful as an artist, he was given permission to dissect human corpses at the hospital Santa Maria Nuova in Florence. Later his dissected in Milan at Hospital Maggiore and in Rome at the hospital Santa Spirito (1st mainland Hospital in Italy). He collaborated with Dr Marcantonio Della Torre for his study from 1510 to 1511.

> I have removed skin from a man who was so shrunk by illness that the muscles were worn down and remained in a state like thin membrane, in such a way that the sinews instead of merging in muscle ended in wide membrane; where the bones were covered by the skin they had very little over their natural size.

In 30 years, Leonardo has dissected many Women and Men corpses from different ages. Together with Marcantonio, he prepared to publish theorical work on anatomy and made more than 200 drawings. However, this book was only published in 1680 (161 years after his death) under heading "Treatise on Painting."

Among the detailed images that Leonardo drew are many studies of Human skeleton. He was the first to describe the double S form of backbone. He also studied the inclination of pelvis and sacrum and stressed that sacrum is not uniform but composed of 5 fused vertebrae. He also studied anatomy of Human foot and its connection to the leg, from these studies he was able to study biomechanics.

Leonardo was a physiologist as well as an anatomist, studying the function of the human Body as well as examining and recording its structure. He dissected and drew the Human skull and cross-sections of the brain, transversal, sagittal and frontal. These drawings may be linked to a search for the census communis, the locus of the human senses, which, by medieval tradition, was located at the exact physical center of the skull.

Leonardo studied internal organs, being the first one to draw Human appendix and the lungs, mesentery, urinary tract, reproductive organs, muscles of cervix and a detailed of cross-section of coitus. He was one of the first ones to draw a scientific representation of the fetus intrautero.

Leonardo studied vascular system and drew a dissected heart in detail. He correctly worked out how heart valves ebb flow of blood, yet he fully didn't fully understand the circulation as he believed that blood was pumped to the muscles where it was consumed. In 2005 a UK heart surgeon, Francis Wells, from papworth Hospital Cambridge, pioneered repair of damaged hearts, using Leonardo's depiction of the opening phase of the mitral valve to operate without changing its diameter allowing a patient to recover fast. Wells told "Leonardo had a depth of appreciation of anatomy and physiology of body – its structure and function – that perhaps overlooked by some."

Leonardo's observational acumen, drawing skills and clarity of deception of bone structure reveals him at his finest as a anatomist. However, his deception of the internal soft tissue of the body are incorrect in many ways, showing that he maintained concepts of anatomy and functioning that were in some cases millennia old, and that his investigation was probably hampered by lack of preservation techniques available at the time. Leonardo's detail drawing of internal organ of a woman reveal many traditional misconceptions.

Leonardo's study of Human anatomy led also to the design of automation which has come to be called Leonardo's robot, which was probably made around the year 1495 but was only reinvented in 1950s.

Comparative Anatomy

Leonardo not only study Human anatomy but also animals. He dissected Cows, birds, horses, dogs, monkeys and frogs comparing in his drawing their anatomical structure with that of human. On one page of his journal he drew 5 profile studies of Horse with its teeth bared in anger and, for comparison a snarling lion and snarling man.

> I have found that in composition of human body with animals' bodies, the organs of sense are duller and coarser… I have seen in lion tribe that the sense of smell is connected with part of brain which come down the nostrils, which form a spacious receptacle for sense of smell, which enters by a great number of cartilaginous vesicles with several passage leading up to where brain, as before said, come down.

In the early 1490s Leonardo was commissioned to create a monument in honor of Francesco Sforza. In his notebooks are a series of plans for an equestrian monument. There are also large number of related anatomical studies of horses. They include several diagrams of a standing horse with the angle and proportion annotated, anatomical studies of a horses' heads, a dozen detailed drawings of hooves and numerous studies of horses rearing.

He studied the topographical anatomy of a bear in detail, making many drawings of its paws. There is also a drawing of the muscles and tendons of the bear's hind feet. Other drawings of interest include the uterus of a pregnant cow, the hindquarters of a decrepit mule and studies of the musculature of a little dog.

Botany

Leonardo wrote:

> All the branches of the tree at every stage of its height when put together are equal in thickness to the trunk.

The science of botany was long established in Leonardo's time, a treatise on the subject having been written as early as 300 BCE. Leonardo's study of plants, resulting in many beautiful drawings in his notebooks, was not to record in diagrammatic form the parts of the plant, but rather, as an artist and observer to record the precise appearance of plants, the manner of growth and the way that individual plants and flowers of a single variety differed from one another.

One such study shows a page with several species of flower of which ten drawings are of wild violets. Along with a drawing of the growing plant and a detail of a leaf, Leonardo has repeatedly drawn single flowers from different angles, with their heads set differently on the stem.

Apart from flowers the notebooks contain many drawings of crop plants including several types of grain and a variety of berries including a detailed study of bramble. There are also water plants such as irises and sedge. His notebooks also direct the artist to observe how light reflects from foliage at different distances and under different atmospheric conditions.

Several the drawings have their equivalents in Leonardo's paintings. An elegant study of a stem of lilies may have been for one of Leonardo's early Annunciation paintings, carried in the hand of the Archangel Gabriel. In both the Annunciation pictures the grass is dotted with blossoming plants.

Geology

As an adult, Leonardo had only 2 childhood memories, one of which finding a cave in Apennines. Although fearing that he might be attacked by wild beast, he ventured in driven "by burning desire to see whether there might be any marvelous thing within."

Leonardo's earliest dated drawing in study of Arnos valley, strong emphasizing its geological features. His notebooks contain landscapes with wealth of geological observation from the regions of both Florence and Milan, often including atmosphere effect such as heavy rainstorm pouring down on town at the foot of mountain range.

It had been observed for many years that strata in mountains often contained bands of sea shells. Conservative science said that these could be explained by the Great Flood described in bible. Leonardo's observation convinced his that this could not possibly be the case.

And a little beyond the sandstone conglomerate, a tufa has been formed, where it turned towards castle Florentino; farther on, the mud was deposited in which the shells lived, and which rose in layers according to the levels at which the turbid Arno Flowed into that sea. And from time to time the bottom of the sea was raised, depositing these shells in layers, as may be seen in the cutting at Colle Gonzoli, laid open by Arno which is wearing way base of it; in which cutting the said layers of shells are very plainly to be seen in clay of bluish color, and various marine objects are found there.

This quotation makes clear the breadth of Leonardo's understanding of geology, including the action of water in creating sedimentary rock, the tectonic action of the Earth in raising the sea bed and the action of erosion in the creation of geographical features.

In Leonardo's earliest paintings we see the remarkable attention given to the small landscapes of the background, with lakes and water, swathed in a misty light. In the larger of the Annunciation paintings is a town on the edge of a lake. Although distant, the mountains can be seen to be scored by vertical strata. This characteristic can be observed in other paintings by Leonardo, and closely resembles the mountains around Lago di Garda and Lago d'Iseo in Northern Italy. It is a feature of both the paintings of The Virgin of the Rocks, which also include caverns of fractured, tumbled, and water-eroded limestone.

Cartography

In the early 16th century maps were rare and often inaccurate. Leonardo produced several extreme accurate maps such as town plan of Imola created in 1502 to win patronage of Cesare Borgia. Borgia was so impressed that he hired him as Military engineer and an architect. Leonardo also produced a map of Chiana valley in Tuscany, which he surveyed, without the benefit of modern equipment, by pacing the distances. In 1515, Leonardo produced map of the Roman Southern coast which is linked to his work for the Vatican and relates to his plans to drain the marshland.

Recent research by Donato Pezzutto suggested that the background landscapes in Leonardo's paintings depict specific locations as aerial view with enhanced depth, employing a technique called cartographic perspective. Pezzutto identifies the location of the Mona Lisa to the Val di Chiana, the Annunciation to the Arno valley, the Madonna of yarnwinder to Adda Valley and the Virgin and child with St Anne to the Sessia Valley.

Leonardo developed several plans for altering the course of the River Arno which flow through Florence. He carefully mapped the river in 1503 work was started on digging 3 new channels to cut off a bend in the river; it was taught this will improve its flow. Several thousand men were involved in this project.

Hydrodynamics

Leonardo wrote:

> All the branches of a water [course] at every
> stage of its course, if they are of equal

rapidly, are equal to the body of the main stream.

Among Leonardo's drawing are many that are studies of the motion of water, the forms taken by fast-flowing water on striking different stream.

Many of these drawings depict the spiraling nature of water. The spiral form had been studied in the art of the Classical era and strict Mathematical proportion had been applied to its use in art and architecture. An awareness of these rules of proportion had been revived in the early Renaissance.

There are several elaborate drawings of curling water over an object placed at diagonal to its course. There are several drawings of water dropping from a height and curling upwards in spiral forms. One such drawing, as well as curling waves, splash and detail of spay and bubbles.

Leonardo's interest manifested itself in the drawing of streams and rivers, the action of water in eroding rocks, and the cataclysmic action of water in floods and tidal waves. The knowledge that he gained from his studies was employed in devising a range of projects, particularly in relation to the Arno River. None of the major works was brought to completion.

Astronomy

Leonardo wrote:

> The earth is not in the center of the Sun's orbit nor at the center of the universe, but in the center of its companion elements, and united with them. And any one standing on the moon, when it and the sun are both beneath us, would see this our earth and the element of water upon it just as we see the moon, and the earth would light it as it lights us.

Much of his studies in this area are often contradictory or said to focus on unimportant events. However, it must be remembered that the telescope was not even in existence during Leonardo's time, though concave and convex lenses were understood and used for vision correction. Some recent claims have been made that Leonardo designed his own telescope, but it seems unlikely he would not have realized the potential for something like this in times of war and made more extensive note of it.

Despite the probable lack of suitable equipment for studying the skies, it was Leonardo who suggested an answer to a question which had been asked since ancient times, that being whether the movement of heavenly bodies produced any sound. His reasoning was that they couldn't, and Leonardo even suggested several possible reasons as to why this would be. We now know his conclusions to be correct.

Alchemy

Claims are sometime made that Leonardo da Vinci was an alchemist. He was trained in Verrocchio's workshop, who according to Vasari, was able alchemist. Leonardo was chemist in so much as that he experimented with different media for suspending paint pigment. In the painting of murals, his experiments resulted in notorious failure with the Last Supper deterioration within century, and the Battle of Anghiari running off the wall. In Leonardo's many pages of notes about artistic processes, there are some that pertain to the use of silver and gold in artworks, information he would have learnt as a student.

Leonardo's scientific process was based mainly upon observation. His practical experiments are also founded in observation rather then belief. Leonardo, who questioned the order of solar system and the deposit of fossil by the Great flood, had very little time for the alchemical quest to turn lead into gold or create a potion that gave external life.

Leonardo said about alchemists:

> The false interpreters of nature declare that quicksilver is the common seed of every metal, not remembering that nature varies the seed according to the variety of the things she desires to produce in the world.

> Old alchemists... have never either by chance or by experiment succeeded in creating the smallest element that can be created by nature; however [they] deserve unmeasured praise for the usefulness of things invented for use of men and would deserve it even more if they had not been the inventors of noxious things like poisons and other similar things which destroy life or mind.

> And many have made a trade of delusions and false miracle, deceiving the stupid multitude.

Mathematic Studies

Perspective

The art of perspective is of such a nature as to make what is flat appear in relief and what is in relief flat.

During the early 15th century, both Brunelleschi and Alberti made studies of linear perspective. In 1436 Alberti published "della Pittura", which includes his findings on linear perspective. Piero della Francesca carried his work forward and by the 1470s several artists were able to produce works of art that demonstrated a full understanding of the principles of linear perspective.

Leonardo studied linear perspective and employed it in his earliest paintings. His use of perspective in 2 Annunciation is darling, as he uses various features such as the corner of a building, a walled garden and path to contrast enclosure and spaciousness.

The unfinished adoration of the Magi was intended to be masterpiece revealing much of Leonardo's knowledge of figures drawing and perspective. There exist several studies that he made, including a detailed study of perspective, showing the complex background of ruined Classical Building that he planned for the left of the picture. In accumulation, Leonardo is created with the first use of anamorphosis, the use of a "perspective" to produce an image that is intelligible only with a curved mirror or from a specific vantage point.

Leonardo wrote:

> Those who are in love with practice without knowledge are like the sailor who gets into a ship without rudder or compass and who never can be certain whether he is going. Practice must always be founded on sound theory, and to this Perspective is the guide and the gateway; and without this nothing can be done well in the matter of drawing.

Geometry

While in Milan in 1496 Leonardo met travelling monk and academic, Luca Pacioli. Under him, Leonardo studied mathematics. Pacioli, who first codified and recorded the double entry system of bookkeeping, had already published a major treatise on mathematical knowledge, collaborated with

Leonardo in production of a book called "De divina proportione" was published in 1509.

>All the problems of perspective are made clear by the five terms of mathematicians, which are: —the point, the line, the angle, the superficies and the solid. The point is unique of its kind. And the point has neither height, breadth, length, nor depth, whence it is to be regarded as indivisible and as having no dimensions in space.

Engineering and Invention

Vasari in lives of the Artists says of Leonardo:

>He made designs for mills, fulling machines and engines that could be driven by water-power... In addition, he used to make models and plans showing how to excavate and tunnel through

mountains without difficulty, so as to pass from one level to another; and he demonstrated how to lift and draw great weights by means of levers, hoists and winches, and ways of cleansing harbors and using pumps to suck up water from great depths.

Practical inventions and projects

Leonardo was a Master of Mechanical principles. He utilized leverage and cantilevering, pulleys, cranks, gears, including angle gears and rack and pinion gears; parallel linkage, lubrication systems and bearings. He understood the principles governing momentum, centripetal force, friction and the aerofoil and applied these to his inventions. His scientific studies remained unpublished with, for example, his manuscripts describing the processes governing friction predating the introduction of Amontons' Laws of Friction by 150 years.

It is impossible to say with any certainty how many or even which of his inventions passed into general and practical use, and thereby had impact over the lives of many people. Among those inventions that are credited with passing into general practical use are the strut bridge, the automated bobbin winder, the rolling mill, the machine for testing the tensile strength of wire and the lens-grinding machine pictured at right. In the lens-grinding machine, the hand rotation of the grinding wheel operates an angle-gear, which rotates a shaft, turning a geared dish in which sits the glass or crystal to be ground. A single action rotates both surfaces at a fixed speed ratio determined by the gear.

As an inventor, Leonardo was not prepared to tell all that he knew:

How by means of a certain machine many people may stay some time under water. How and why I do not describe my method of remaining under water, or how long I can stay without eating; and I do not publish nor divulge these by reason of the evil nature of men who would use them as means of destruction at the bottom of the sea, by sending ships to the bottom, and sinking them together with the men in them. And although I will impart others, there is no danger in them; because the mouth of the tube, by which you breathe, is above the water supported on bags of corks

Clocks

The Codex Madrid shed a great deal of light on Leonardo's fascination with clocks. This is not surprising considering he lived during a period when clocks were being greatly improved, and those used were often of massive size presenting interesting challenges to the engineer.

It was just prior to Leonardo's time that clock makers first started to explore using springs as an alternative to weights for powering clocks. They developed the fuse to keep the force of the spring even as it wound down and this was usually controlled by gut or chain. The down side of this was the tendency for these items to stretch or break, making them unreliable. Leonardo worked on a clock spring equalizer, but no one has ever tested his ideas, so whether it would have worked remains unknown.

Leonardo not only drew all the parts of clocks, he used diamonds and semi-precious stones in his mechanisms. He even invented and used an alarm clock in which water flowed in a thin stream from one receptacle to another. When the second receptacle was full a system of gears and levers raised Leonardo's feet into the air.

Cranes

Many of Leonardo's civil machines were labor-saving devices and these included several cranes and devices to ease the problems of lifting.

He designed two automatic release mechanisms which were kept closed by the weight of the loads. As soon as the weight was relieved by contact with the ground the hooks uncoupled. The mechanisms were drawn side-by-side with Leonardo noting that the one on the right was the better of the two as the weighted hook on the other could be jammed by encountering the load.

His twin cranes were probably designed with quarrying in mind, and they allow huge blocks of stone to be shifted quickly and with relative ease. As one crane loaded a stone block from the quarry face the other would discharge its load. The entire rig would then turn around, so the process could be repeated with the second crane unloading while the first reloaded.

Leonardo also designed a travelling crane which was mounted on a small trolley and balanced with guide wires. It revolved on a pivot and was well designed for lifting heavy weights without being cumbersome. This crane would have been of use in the construction of tall buildings and its design was quite sound.

Most of Leonardo's machines were never built in his lifetime. Indeed, many could not have been built due to the lack of suitable parts. It is particularly interesting, therefore, that modern engineers who have built many of his designs managed to make perfect working models. The one downfall that has been observed was the use of too many, or too few, cogs and springs. Some people have suggested that this was deliberate and an attempt by Leonardo to prevent the theft of his projects, most of which were quite feasible. Most Leonardo's ideas were rediscovered centuries after his death.

Spit

The automated roasting spit is a design which has a perfectly practical application and is quite simple. Leonardo did not actually invent this idea, but he drew illustrations which show he studied its operation and how the draught from different sized fires produced a varying result during the roasting of the meat. A hot fire has a stronger draught and so a roast brown more evenly.

Leonardo wrote:

> "the roast will turn slow or fast depending on whether the fire is small and strong."

Lifting Jack

Leonardo's lifting jack is not that dissimilar from the jacks used with modern vehicles. Made up of reducing gears, a rack and a crank handle, it would have been of a great deal of use in Leonardo's day. We do not know if this was an invention by Leonardo, a modification of a piece of equipment, or simply a detailed sketch of equipment already in general use.

Textile

Leonardo's textile machines are among his lesser-known pieces, however he showed great foresight in this area and designed clipping machines, automatic spindles, shearing machines and two rope-twisting machines which appear in Codex Atlanticus. The more complicated of these spins and twists fifteen strands simultaneously.

Of interest is his fabric stretcher which made it possible to achieve a nearly industrial output when several machines were used together. The fabric was stretched on a wooden frame and then automatically cut with two gigantic shears. This design was to reappear in England during the eighteenth century. At this time, it caused grave problems as it replaced so many workers large numbers faced unemployment.

Robot

This is one of Leonardo's least-known designs and he probably developed it during his extensive studies and dissections of the human body. The robot is thought to have been designed just prior to the period of the Last Supper; this would put it at around 1495. It was probably the first ever design for a humanoid robot, and if built, was most certainly the first ever manufactured. The finished robot drawings are among some 14,000 pages of Leonardo's work which remain lost to us, and experts have no indication that this machine progressed beyond Leonardo's initial sketches.

It wasn't until the 1950s that a professor from the University of California suggested some of Leonardo's designs could be for a robot. A further forty years passed before the components of a system for automatically controlling limb movements was identified among the sketches.

This led the Florence-based Institute and Museum of the History of Science to develop computer models designed to establish the feasibility of Leonardo's sketches. These simulations clearly confirmed that the drawings were for a mechanical robot.

It is now obvious that Leonardo designed his robot to open and close its jaw sit up, wave its arms, and move its head. Though uncertainty exists about sound it may use automated drums. The mechanical man was dressed in a suit of armor from the late fifteenth century.

We still do not know what device Leonardo planned to use to activate his robot, but it was most likely water or weights.

Printing press

Well into the seventeenth century presses remained crude and they had progressed little. At the time Leonardo was born Gutenburg had just invented movable type and Leonardo's press was not a new design; his contribution consisted of suggesting improvements on an existing system. One of Leonardo's modifications was a double thread which would serve to increase the travel of the press for each turn made of the lever. It appears Leonardo intended to publish his information on work done in this area, but it was not until 132 years after his death that this was to happen.

Parachute

Leonardo was very specific in his 1483 design for a parachute:

> "if a man had a tent made of linen, of which all the apertures have been stopped up, and it be twelve braccia [21 feet] across and twelve feet in depth, he will be able to throw himself down from any great height without sustaining any injury."

Unlike modern parachutes, his design was quite rigid and had poles running down from the apex of the canopy. In normal circumstances this type of design would be prone to oscillations, however Leonardo's plan had the man hanging from his arms and it was thought this would reduce the problem.

Over five hundred years after Leonardo drew his sketch, his theories were tested out when Adrian Nicholas of Britain used Leonardo's parachute during a skydive. Three months were spent building the chute, using wood and canvas. Data equipment was attached, and the jump made in ideal weather over Mpumalanga in South Africa. Adrian Nichols commented that:

> "From my perspective, I just saw this canvas material billowing in the wind like the sails of an ancient sailing boat," Nicholas says. "And I just hung there in space. There was no oscillation, no rotation or gyration or anything. And I flew for ages and ages and ages. You could see people in the fields all around waving and shouting. It was wonderful. Absolutely wonderful."

A traditional parachute was used for the landing as Leonardo's chute, though it gave a lovely ride, could not be steered and depended upon for a safe landing. It did, however, land nearby and gently enough that all the recording equipment remained undamaged.

Unfortunately, Leonardo cannot claim to have influenced the modern-day parachute as his design remained undiscovered until the nineteenth century. Modern parachutes are based on parasols whereas Leonardo's is based upon the tent.

Land Vehicles

Leonardo devised many vehicles, both for land and water, for convenience, and use in war. One of his most interesting designs was for a horseless carriage. This was a very basic system involving a platform on wheels, the front ones being articulated, and several coiled springs which drove a set of gears. As each spring was released the driver was required to wind up another one, thus providing (semi) continuous propulsion for his vehicle. But like many of Leonardo's flying machines, the demands on the operator didn't just stop there. He also needed to steer the 'car' using a small rudder-wheel.

Leonardo's drawings for this machine are sketchy when it comes to the spring system and it is thought he could not find a way to overcome the problem of connecting the springs to the wheels. He did make clear depictions of the transmission and this contains a differential which enabled each wheel to turn at a slightly different speed when corning. Many early motor cars lacked this important detail, so it is fascinating to see it in Leonardo's design.

Other wheeled devices developed by Leonardo measured distance (odometers). Each time the wheel completed a revolution a pebble would drop down to a box. The number if pebbles provided the measurement of distance. He later improved this by using a gearing system that meant a pebble would drop only once each mile. This led to a pedometer which could be used on either man or horse and measured the number of steps taken using a pendulum which rested on the thigh.

The bicycle was discovered during the restoration of the Codex Atlanticus. Found on the back of one of the pages, some people originally attributed to Leonardo, however there is now considerable doubt about this. In design it was very similar to our modern bicycles, having handlebars, pedals, and using chain drive. The designer envisaged it as being made from wood. A weak point in the design is the steering system which looks awkward and impractical. It is now considered likely that this drawing was done by a student of Leonardo's, as were several other newly recovered pieces found during the restoration, Perhaps the student had seen a similar item in Leonardo's studio or drawn by the master himself.

But the bicycle may be even more recent than this. During the 1960's Codex Atlanticus was entrusted to a group of monks for examination and restoration. In 1974, the leader of the group announced the discovery of the bicycle among some glued and folded sheets of paper.

This was contradicted by an art historian who had looked at the same papers in 1961. He had not unglued the sheets but had examined them under bright lights. His conclusion was there were two unconnected circles between the sheets, and that was all. Confirmation of whether the bicycle is a hoax would require expert analysis, and these sheets have already been coated in a protective plastic to prevent further deterioration.

Water Craft

Leonardo designed a range of water craft, from floating dredgers, to paddle boats, to semi-submersibles intended for use in times of war. He started his studies by drawing the shapes of fishes rationalizing that nature had designed these to move smoothly through the water.

Sludge and silt needed removing from canals, rivers and harbors. In one design for a dredger Leonardo mounted large toothed wheel between two barges, along similar lines to a catamaran. A crank or winch turned the wheel, and four attached scoops rotated collecting the sludge, then discharging it into another barge. This barge was only suitable for depths of a few feet.

For deep dredging, of the type required in a harbor, Leonardo considered a completely different option. A dozen anchors would secure this barge to the bottom; such a large number would be needed to hold the barge against the drag of large boxlike bucket beneath it. The bucket had spikes at the open end and perforations to allow for the free flow of water. This 'plough' (Leonardo's term) was then to be dragged out to the required spot and the bucket moved along the seabed, lifted out using a windlass, and discharged into another barge.

The crank-operated paddle boat shown here is just one of many similar designs to be found in Codex Atlanticus. It had shovel-shaped paddles which were turned by a crank system. To assist the operator Leonardo planned a gearing system which caused the paddle wheel to turn at a faster rate than the crank. But the lack of our modern power systems severely hampered Leonardo in this area. He only had wind, water, or muscle power to work with so was forced to try and design ways they could be made to work more efficiently.

One solution he tried was treadle power. As the treadles are raised and lowered they operate a belt around a central drum. This, in turn, is geared to toothed wheels which drive the paddles. This is a very practical design only required the addition of a steering device to be useful. It is considered that this is about as far as Leonardo could go with the technology available to him at the time.

Water pumps

Leonardo did much work with water pumps and wells. During Leonardo's time man had already built up considerable knowledge in these areas and Verrocchio was an experienced hydraulic engineer; it was him who first introduced Leonardo to the subject.

Canal

An excellent drawing of a canal system has been dated to 1480-1485. It displays the canal complete with two sets of locks built alongside weirs. Houses for those operating the locks stand alongside the canal and boats are shown making their way through it. Another area of this sheet shows the gates in detail.

Leonardo was consulted regarding canal engineering and it is known he was responsible for the design of a canal which would have linked Milan to the sea. It seems Leonardo intended to dig some vast canals -- up to 60 feet wide and 21 feet deep. He designed sets of hinged gates that met at an angle and formed a watertight joint caused by the pressure of water on their mitred edges. In 1497 six locks were built using Leonardo's system and it is still in very common use today.

Bridge and hydraulics

Leonardo's study of the motion of water led him to design machinery that utilized its force. Much of his work on hydraulics was for Ludovico il Moro. Leonardo wrote to Ludovico describing his skills and what he could build:

> ...very light and strong bridges that can easily be carried, with which to pursue, and sometimes flee from, the enemy; and others safe and

indestructible by fire or assault, easy and convenient to transport and place into position.

Among his projects in Florence was one to divert the course of the Arno, to flood Pisa. Fortunately, this was too costly to be carried out. He also surveyed Venice and came up with a plan to create a movable dyke for the city's protection against invaders.

In 1502, Leonardo produced a drawing of a single span 240 m (720 ft) bridge as part of a civil engineering project for Ottoman Sultan Beyazid II of Istanbul. The bridge was intended to span an inlet at the mouth of the Bosphorus known as the Golden Horn. Beyazid did not pursue the project, because he believed that such a construction was impossible. Leonardo's vision was resurrected in 2001 when a smaller bridge based on his design was constructed in Norway.

War machines

Leonardo's letter to Ludovico il Moro assured him:

> When a place is besieged I know how to cut off water from the trenches and construct an infinite variety of bridges, mantlets and scaling ladders, and other instruments pertaining to sieges. I also have types of mortars that are very

convenient and easy to transport.... when a place cannot be reduced by the method of bombardment either because of its height or its location, I have methods for destroying any fortress or other stronghold, even if it be founded upon rock. .... If the engagement be at sea, I have many engines of a kind most efficient for offence and defense, and ships that can resist cannons and powder.

In Leonardo's notebooks there is an array of war machines which includes a vehicle to be propelled by two men powering crank shafts. Although the drawing itself looks quite finished, the mechanics were apparently not fully developed because, if built as drawn, the vehicle would never progress in a forward direction. In a BBC documentary, a military team built the machine and changed the gears to make the machine work. It has been suggested that Leonardo deliberately left this error in the design, to prevent it from being put to practice by unauthorized people. Another machine, propelled by horses with a pillion rider, carries in front of it four scythes mounted on a revolving gear, turned by a shaft driven by the wheels of a cart behind the horses.

Leonardo's notebooks also show cannons which he claimed, "to hurl small stones like a storm with the smoke of these causing great terror to the enemy, and great loss and confusion." He also designed an enormous crossbow. Following his detailed drawing, one was constructed by the British Army, but could not be made to fire successfully. In 1481 Leonardo designed a breech-loading, water cooled cannon with three racks of barrels allowed the re-loading of one rack while another was being fired and thus maintaining continuous fire power. The "fan type" gun with its array of horizontal barrels allowed for a wide scattering of shot.

Leonardo was the first to sketch the wheel-lock musket c. 1500 AD (the precedent of the flintlock musket which first appeared in Europe by 1547), although as early as the 14th century the Chinese had used a flintlock 'steel wheel' to detonate land mines.

While Leonardo was working in Venice, he drew a sketch for an early diving suit, to be used in the destruction of enemy ships entering Venetian waters. A suit was constructed for a BBC documentary using pigskin treated with fish oil to repel water. The head was covered by a helmet with two eyeglasses at the front. A breathing tube of bamboo with pigskin joints was attached to the back of the helmet and connected to a float of cork and wood. When the scuba divers tested the suit, they found it to be a workable precursor to a modern diving suit, the cork float acting as a compressed air chamber when submerged. His inventions were very futuristic which meant they were very expensive and proved not to be useful.

Flight

In Leonardo's infancy a hawk had once hovered over his cradle. Recalling this incident, Leonardo saw it as prophetic.

> An object offers as much resistance to the air as the air does to the object. You may see that the beating of its wings against the air supports a heavy eagle in the highest and rarest atmosphere, close to the sphere of elemental fire. Again, you may see the air in motion over the sea, fill the swelling sails and drive heavily laden ships. From these instances, and the reasons given, a man with wings large enough and duly connected might learn to overcome the resistance of the air, and by conquering it, succeed in subjugating it and rising above it.

The desire to fly is expressed in the many studies and drawings. His later journals contain a detailed study of the flight of birds and several different designs for wings based in structure upon those of bats which he described as being less heavy because of the impenetrable nature of the membrane. There is a legend that Leonardo tested the flying machine on Monte Ceceri with one of his apprentices, and that the apprentice fell and broke his leg. Experts Martin Kemp and Liana Bortolon agree that there is no evidence of such a test, which is not mentioned in his journals.

One design that he produced shows a flying machine to be lifted by a man-powered rotor. It would not have worked since the body of the craft itself would have rotated in the opposite direction to the rotor.

While he designed a number of man powered flying machines with mechanical wings that flapped, he also designed a parachute and a light hang glider which could have flown.

Musical Instruments

The viola organista was an experimental musical instrument invented by Leonardo da Vinci. It was the first bowed keyboard instrument (of which any record has survived) ever to be devised.

Leonardo's original idea, as preserved in his notebooks of 1488–1489 and in the drawings in the Codex Atlanticus, was to use one or more wheels, continuously rotating, each of which pulled a looping bow, rather like a fanbelt in an automobile engine, and perpendicular to the instrument's strings.

Inventions Became Reality

In the late 20th century, interest in Leonardo's invention escalated. There have been projects which have sought to turn diagrams on paper turned into working models. One of the factor is awareness, that although in 15th and 16th centuries Leonardo had available a limited range of materials, modern technologies advancements have made available a number of robust material of light-weight which might turn Leonardo's design into reality. This is particularly the case with his design for flying machines.

A difficulty met in creation of models is that often Leonardo had not entirely though the mechanics of a machine before he drew it, or else he used a sort of graphic shorthand, simply not bothering to draw a gear or a lever at a point where one is essential in order to make a machine function. This lack of refinement of mechanical details can cause considerable confusion. Thus, many models that are created, such as some of those on display at Clos Luce, Leonardo's home in France, do not work, but would work, with a little mechanical tweaking.

Exhibition

- Leonardo da Vinci gallery at Museo Nazionale della Scienza e della Tecnologia "Leonardo da Vinci" in Milan; permanent exhibition, the biggest collection of Leonardo's projects and inventions.

- The Victoria and Albert Museum, London, held an exhibition called "Leonardo da Vinci: Experience, Experiment and Design" in 2006

- Logitech Museum

- "The Da Vinci Machines Exhibition" was held in a pavilion in the Cultural Forecourt, at South Bank, Brisbane, Queensland, Australia in 2009. The exhibits shown were on loan from the Museum of Leonardo da Vinci, Florence, Italy.

Leonardo da Vinci's Artwork

Fifteen artworks are generally attributed either in whole or in large part to him. Most are paintings on panel, with the remainder being a mural, a large drawing on paper, and two works in the early stages of preparation. The authorship of several paintings traditionally attributed to Leonardo is disputed. Two major works are known only as copies. Works are regularly attributed to Leonardo with varying degrees of credibility. None of Leonardo's paintings are signed. The attributions here draw on the opinions of various scholars.

The small number of surviving paintings is due in part to Leonardo's frequently disastrous experimentation with new techniques and his chronic procrastination. Nevertheless, these few works together with his notebooks, which contain drawings, scientific diagrams, and his thoughts on the nature of painting, comprise a contribution to later generations of artists rivalled only by that of his contemporary, Michelangelo.

Old Age & Death

From September 1513 to 1516, under Pope Leo X, Leonardo spent much of his time living in the Belvedere in the Vatican in Rome, where Raphael and Michelangelo were both active at the time. In October 1515, King Francis I of France recaptured Milan. On 19 December, Leonardo was present at the meeting of Francis I and Pope Leo X, which took place in Bologna. Leonardo was commissioned to make for Francis a mechanical lion that could walk forward then open its chest to reveal a cluster of lilies. In 1516, he entered Francis' service, being given the use of the manor house Clos Lucé, now a public museum, near the king's residence at the royal Château d'Amboise.

Leonardo died at Clos Lucé, on 2 May 1519 at the age of 67. The cause is generally stated to be recurrent stroke; this diagnosis is consistent with accounts of the state of Leonardo's alleged remains as described in 1863. Francis I had become a close friend. Vasari describes Leonardo as lamenting on his deathbed, full of repentance, that "he had offended against God and men by failing to practice his art as he should have done." Vasari also records that the king held Leonardo's head in his arms as he died, although this story, portrayed in romantic paintings by Ingres, Ménageot and other French artists, as well as by Angelica Kauffman, may be legend rather than fact. Vasari states that in his last days, Leonardo sent for a priest to make his confession and to receive the Holy Sacrament. In accordance with his will, sixty beggars followed his casket. Melzi was the principal heir and executor, receiving, as well as money, Leonardo's paintings, tools, library and personal effects. Leonardo also remembered his other long-time pupil and companion, Salai, and his servant Battista di Vilussis, who each received half of Leonardo's vineyards. His brothers received land, and his serving woman received a black cloak "of good stuff" with a fur edge. Leonardo da Vinci was buried in the Collegiate Church of Saint-Florentin in Château d'Amboise in France.

Location of Remain

Leonardo's remains were originally interred in the Collegiate Church of Saint-Florentin at the Château d'Amboise in the Loire Valley. However, following the church's destruction in 1802, the whereabouts of Leonardo's remains became subject to dispute. While excavating the site in 1863, the poet Arsène Houssaye found a partially-complete skeleton and stone fragments. The unusually large skull led Houssaye to conclude he had located the remains of Leonardo, which were re-interred in their present location of the Chapel of Saint-Hubert, also at the Château d'Amboise. Reflecting doubts about the attribution, a plaque above the tomb states that the remains are only "presumed" to be those of Leonardo. In 2016, it was announced that DNA tests were to be conducted to investigate the veracity of the attribution.

Epilogue

So Leonardo da vinci is not only a Painter who painted The Mona lisa but also a Legend who was excellent in most of the professions you can think of!

THE END